LC 25-2010

OWLS

OWLS

MICHAEL GEORGE

THE CHILD'S WORLD

PHOTO RESEARCH

Charles Rotter/Gary Lopez Productions

PHOTO CREDITS

Joe McDonald: front cover, 6, 9, 13, 14, 22
COMSTOCK/Art Gingert: back cover, 2, 27, 28
Tom & Pat Leeson: 10, 18
COMSTOCK/Phyllis Greenberg: 17, 21
COMSTOCK/Bonnie Kamin: 24
COMSTOCK/Denver Bryan: 31

Distributed to schools and libraries in the United States by
ENCYCLOPAEDIA BRITANNICA EDUCATIONAL CORP.
310 South Michigan Avenue
Chicago, Illinois 60604

Library of Congress Cataloging-in-Publication Data
George, Michael, 1964-
Owls / by Michael George.
p. cm.
Summary: Introduces the physical characteristics,
behavior, and life cycle of owls.
ISBN 0-89565-837-2
1. Owls--Juvenile literature. [1. Owls.] I. Title.
QL696.S8G46 1992
598.9'7--dc20
91-34736
CIP
AC

Dedicated to loggers who respect the lives of other animals.

Do you think of owls as large, evil birds swooping out of the sky on halloween night? Maybe there is a witch on a broomstick following close behind. Or perhaps you think of the wise old owl, giving advice after a thoughtful stare.

These images of the owl are shared by many people, but none of them are actually true. Owls are not evil creatures that hang out with witches. Nor are they wiser than robins, sparrows, or any other bird. However, the truth about owls is as fascinating as the stories you may have heard.

There are about 140 different kinds of owls. They vary greatly in size. Eagle owls are the largest of all. They have six-foot wingspans and weigh as much as house cats. However, not all owls are giants. Some kinds of owls, like the screech owl in this picture, are not much bigger than other birds.

Regardless of their size, owls look different from all other birds. They have round faces covered with soft, fluffy feathers. Their faces are outlined by two large circles, called *facial disks*. Owls also have big, round eyes and sharp, curved bills.

Owls live on every continent except Antarctica. They can be found in frozen snow country and in tropical jungles. Some owls live on open grasslands, while others live in dense forests. There are even some owls that live in big cities.

The snowy owl in this picture lives in the Far North, on the cold arctic tundra. It has a thick, warm coat of feathers. The white feathers help the owl blend in with its snowy surroundings. This protects the owl from enemies and helps it sneak up on prey.

Most owls live far from the frozen tundra. Owls that live in tropical jungles usually have small bodies and short wings. This makes it easy for them to fly through the jungle's thick vegetation. This long-eared owl has much larger wings than its relatives in the tropics. It lives in northern forests where there is plenty of room to fly.

Although owls can be quite large, they are rarely seen by people or other animals. Most owls are active at night and sleep during the day. They often nestle close to tree trunks on high branches. Their feathers blend in with the trees, so they are very hard to see.

This is a picture of a great horned owl. Like many other owls, great horned owls have long feathers that stick up on top of their heads. These feathers are called *ear tufts*, but they are not the owl's actual ears. An owl's ears are hidden beneath its feathers. Even so, owls have excellent hearing.

Owls also have keen eyesight. They can even see in the dark. In fact, owls have the best night vision of any creature. They can see things in the dark that even a cat would miss.

An owl's eyes face straight ahead, not to the side like those of other birds. The owl must turn its head to see something to the side. Luckily, an owl's neck is very flexible. An owl can turn its head so far that it can see backward. Sometimes it looks like an owl's head can spin all the way around!

Owls use their keen hearing and eyesight to hunt for food. Most owls eat insects, small rodents, birds, or snakes. Large owls sometimes attack squirrels, rabbits, or even young deer.

Most owls hunt only at night. An owl sits on a tree branch and watches and listens. When it spots something to eat, the owl swoops down from its perch, almost without a sound. Soft feathers on the owl's wings allow it to fly very quietly. In an instant, the owl is on top of its victim. It extends its sharp claws, called *talons,* and snatches up its meal.

After catching dinner, the owl carries its meal back to its perch. Owls do not have teeth, so they cannot chew their food. They must swallow their prey whole, bones and all. If the meal is large, the owl tears it into pieces with its sharp bill.

Most owls hunt in the same area their entire lives. They patrol their territories to keep out other birds. Owls viciously defend their nests and their young. They use their sharp talons and beaks to slash at any intruder, even a person.

Unlike most other birds, owls do not construct fancy nests. Some owls nest in holes in trees, adding a few twigs and leaves. Burrowing owls, like the two in this picture, build their nests beneath the ground.

Baby owls, called *owlets*, hatch from eggs in the spring. Newborn owlets do not look much like their parents. They have small wings and are covered with soft, fluffy down. Adult feathers begin to replace the fuzzy down when the owlets are two or three weeks old. Soon afterward, the mother owl teaches her young to fly. The young owls leave their parents when they are a few months old.

Although owls patrol the woods at night, they are not evil creatures that people need to fear. In fact, we should be happy they are around. By hunting mice and other pests, owls help make the world a safer place to live. So if you hear an owl's distinctive whoo, hoo, hoo, don't be alarmed. The owl is probably stalking a small rodent—not you!

THE CHILD'S WORLD
NATUREBOOKS

Wildlife Library

Alligators	Musk-oxen
Arctic Foxes	Octopuses
Bald Eagles	Owls
Beavers	Penguins
Birds	Polar Bears
Black Widows	Primates
Camels	Rattlesnakes
Cheetahs	Reptiles
Coyotes	Rhinoceroses
Dogs	Seals and Sea Lions
Dolphins	Sharks
Elephants	Snakes
Fish	Spiders
Giraffes	Tigers
Insects	Walruses
Kangaroos	Whales
Lions	Wildcats
Mammals	Wolves
Monarchs	Zebras

Space Library

Earth	The Moon
Mars	The Sun

Adventure Library

Glacier National Park	Yellowstone National Park
The Grand Canyon	Yosemite